SPATULA SUCCESS

BY "PANINI" PETE BLOHME

Published in Mobile, Alabama, by PP Publishing LLC,
an imprint of Back Porch Publishing LLC.

ISBN 979-8-9872693-0-5

Editor: Stephanie Glines
Cover Design: Magge Gagliardi
Layout: Virginia Mathers

Printed in the United States of America

IF FLAVORTOWN HAD A HALL OF FAME, CHEF PETE BLOHME WOULD BE IN THERE.

Since 2008, when I first stepped into his Fairhope, Alabama, shop, "Panini Pete" has been a reliable and trusted friend, a celebrated DDD ambassador, and a proven "good guy" in the hospitality business. From his roots as a CIA trained chef to his travels around the world in support of our troops, Pete's life and career have thrived as true examples of that old mantra "hard work pays off." And to get there, and I've seen this personally, Pete's never let an opportunity be wasted, regardless of whether for his gain or somebody else's. So, what I'm saying is, Panini's got a point...check out *Spatula Success* and see how you too can make the most of what's thrown at you.

– GUY FIERI
Celebrity Chef & Emmy Award-Winning
Food Network Host

"Panini" Pete Blohme's memoir, *Spatula Success*, should be required reading for all business owners but especially for dreamers who want to own a restaurant! Narrating his journey from a kid who liked to cook to the owner of many restaurants and other businesses, Pete shares the primary ingredients of the recipe for success: true hospitality, using the freshest food for his scratch kitchen, developing a great team, investing consistent time and energy in every detail, loving what he does, paying back to his community, and "DIGGING DEEP" around every corner. This is a delicious read simmering with heart, humor, passion, and bullseye focus. Like an encounter with the man himself, *Spatula Success* will leave you smiling big and craving a small bite of the sweetness Pete brings to life and everything he does.

– LUCY BUFFETT
Owner of LuLu's
Gulf Shores, Destin & North Myrtle Beach

I learned early in life that inspiration comes in many forms. Having role models has been a major key to my success professionally and personally. Pete doesn't know it, but he's one of those guys I've been watching really close. The energy, passion and love he has for his craft and others motivates the hell out of me. *Spatula Success* gives me a closer look at how he does it. That and some great recipes!

– TERRY JAMES
Host Lex & Terry,
Nationally-Syndicated Morning Show

I have known "Panini" Pete Blohme for several decades now. My wife Lynne, a native Alabamian and also an alumnus of the CIA has too. While we have always been impressed by his energy, enthusiasm and entrepreneurial zeal, over the years we have happily watched "Panini" grow and develop as a talented chef and savvy businessperson. Pete has thrived where others have failed. He has also overcome seemingly insurmountable obstacles—all while making many people happy and giving back to his community. For Pete, that means not just the good folks of Alabama's Gulf Coast, but also members of the US military, and of course, his alma mater—The Culinary Institute of America (CIA). Pete has been a key leader on the college's Alumni Council, and the groups many contributions to the CIA have made a difference. Through Pete's personal and professional development, he has gained wisdom—some of which he is sharing (along with several of his signature recipes) in *Spatula Success*. I'm confident that you will enjoy and gain from it.

– DR. TIM RYAN
President, The Culinary Institute of America

Panini Pete's recipes go way beyond cooking, offering life skills as well as advice for giving back. Everyone who reads *Spatula Success* will take away a pearl of wisdom!

–LYNNE WEEMS RYAN
Chef, Queen Bee of Chefs to Dine For, Alabama native

I KNOW WHAT YOU'RE THINKING. *Spatula Success? How could a spatula possibly relate to me and my life, my relationships, my family and my career?* Good question. And believe me, I fully understand your confusion. It didn't make sense to me either until that very moment when, well … it made perfect sense.

A few years back, I had the honor of cooking for the men and women of our U.S. Navy aboard the USS Enterprise. After a long day of serving up about 3,500 meals to the sailors on the "Big E," I walked out on to the flight deck and took in the incredible sight of the jets launching from the aircraft carrier.

It was a surreal moment for me, and I thought, *"How did I get here?"* How did a small-town chef and panini shop owner get to this amazing moment and so many other once-in-a-lifetime opportunities over the years?

It was in that moment of reflection that it hit me. As I looked back over the course of my life and career, I realized that I had not arrived here by chance. It wasn't some fate of good fortune or superstar talent on my part that brought me to where I am today.

You see, the little things matter. While many of us spend our lives waiting and hoping for the next "big break" to propel us into the future we're dreaming of, the secret to living a life of abundance is found in the everyday grind. It's the seemingly small decisions and actions that, multiplied over time, lay the solid foundation for building a successful and fulfilling life.

• • •

I started working in the restaurant industry at the age of fourteen and never really stopped. It was a fun and fulfilling gig, but I never considered the food business as anything more than a summer and weekend job.

I was thinking of joining the Armed Forces after high school graduation when my father met a guy who taught hospitality management at Broward Community College in Fort Lauderdale, Florida, where we lived at the time. I was a little intrigued at the idea, so I signed up for classes.

At the same time, I was also fortunate enough to be hired part time in the kitchen at 15th Street Fisheries working under restaurant and hospitality giant Mike Hurst. Mike was a professor of hospitality management at Florida International University, a great operator, a master marketer, and an ambassador for our industry like no other. Looking back, he was the best boss that I ever had.

After the first year at BCC, once my restaurant and hospitality courses were completed, I signed up to take the required core classes like English and Speech and World History, and pretty quickly (okay, immediately) lost interest and dropped out.

I doubled down in the kitchen at "The Fish," as we affectionately called it, and soon was introduced to the CIA. No, not that CIA—the prestigious Culinary Institute of America in Hyde Park, New York. It's the Harvard of cooking schools. Mind you, this was long before the days of the "celebrity chefs" culture. There was no Food Network or Cooking Channel in the early '80s. Culinary school was not a common career choice at the time, and there was definitely no stardom associated with becoming a chef.

Back then, it was difficult to get accepted to CIA. It required several years of experience in quality kitchens and stellar letters of recommendation. And, if you were lucky enough to be accepted, there was typically an 18 to 24-month waiting period. But I decided to go for it, and that's where my journey to becoming a professional chef really started.

I was accepted into CIA and put on an 18-month waiting list. I contacted the school and enthusiastically expressed my gratitude at the opportunity I had just been given, and I told them that if any openings or cancelations came about, I could be there at a moment's notice. My eagerness must have caught their attention because just three months later, I was in! That little bit of extra effort paid off.

After two years of perfect attendance (yes, you read that right), I graduated from CIA and was awarded two fellowships. Fast forward to today and to a culinary career that has spanned over forty years, the first twenty of which were spent learning from some of the best in the food industry. I worked in kitchens at every level—high-volume establishments, regional chains, small independents, college campuses (Roll Tide!) and even cruise ships—before opening my own restaurant in 2006.

Over the past sixteen years, I've built a restaurant company and hospitality brand that today operates four award-winning establishments on the Gulf Coast. I've headlined with Guy Fieri on his Live Road Show performing in 25-plus Road Shows and been featured on a host of Food Network shows such as *Diners, Drive-Ins and Dives*; *Guy's Grocery Games*; *Guy's Big Bite* and *The Great Food Truck Race with Tyler Florence,* as well as CMT's *Sweet Home Alabama.*

My career has opened doors to new ventures for me including consulting, real estate investing, podcasting, writing, and traveling the world as a founding member of a non-profit organization that entertains and cooks for our troops. Oh, and did I mention I recently opened a barber shop?

I don't say all of that to pat myself on the back or to rattle off my resume to try to impress, but to share some of my background in hopes that, first, you'll place enough confidence in me to continue reading. (You know... in case you're still wondering *who in the world is this Panini Pete guy and why should I listen to anything he has to say?*)

And, secondly, because I want to provide some context, so you understand that none of this was an overnight success. The philosophy found in this book is the culmination of a lifetime of personal experiences that include both wins and losses, successes and failures. True success is built one day at a time by paying attention to the small details that others often disregard. It's a principle I first learned in the kitchen and then discovered that it worked in every part of life.

TRUE
SUCCESS
IS BUILT
ONE DAY
AT A
TIME

MANY PROFESSIONS AND TRADES REQUIRE SPECIFIC TOOLS TO GET THE JOB DONE.

A chef's "toolbox" or knife wrap is no exception. A chef has every kind of knife, spoon, scraper, peeler, flipper, turner, shucker, grater, strainer, blender, slicer, dicer, and tweezer you can imagine. And in each category of utensils, there are dozens or sometimes even hundreds of variations.

Just take knives for example. There's a chef knife, filet knife, paring knife, tourne knife, sushi knife, serrated knife, and prime rib slicer, just to name a few. Each tool, and every variation thereof, is designed to do a specific thing with more ease and precision than a less specialized tool.

But of all the finest and fanciest culinary gadgets and cooking gizmos I've used in my career, it's the most basic and low-tech of these utensils that has served me the most. You guessed it—it's the spatula. Just

SPATULAS
ELIMINATE
A MEASURE
OF WASTE

a small section of rubber or silicone attached to the end of a wooden or plastic handle. Now, within the world of spatulas there are variations of shapes and sizes, even heat-resistant ones to be used safely in hot pans. But the fundamental purpose of the spatula is almost exclusively this: *to eliminate a measure of waste.*

When I was at CIA back in the '80s, we were taught that a restaurant's success would likely be determined by controlling and eliminating excessive waste. That's the "make it or break it" in the food industry. Our instructors taught us that trash cans are "lined with gold." Always check for waste, unused product, improperly prepped items, they'd say.

Proper yields and controlling waste are paramount. You can be the latest and greatest restaurant in town with an award-winning chef and exceptional staff but still fail miserably by wasting precious product.

You'll likely find a spatula in most home kitchens, too. But how many mayonnaise, jelly, and peanut butter jars are tossed in the trash every day still coated with plenty of yummy goodness? Or just think of how many times we place batter bowls, blenders, or food processors in the sink to rinse away the remaining deliciousness down the drain.

On the surface, these little remnants of seemingly insignificant dabs and dollops don't appear to matter at all. But when you understand and embrace the principle that the spatula teaches, you will begin to discover the secret ingredient to an abundant life is really no secret at all. It's in using every bit of resource at your disposal. Not just in the kitchen but, as you'll see, in every area of your life.

It could be that the solution to the problem you are facing … the answer you've been searching for … the tools you need to achieve your greatness, to reach your full potential, and to take hold of everything life has in store for you, is right under your nose. Yes, it's possible, even likely, the pathway to get you to your "pinch yourself" moment is right in front of you, undervalued and ignored. Think about it. What are you overlooking?

Of course, getting to the next level will require hard work, a good plan, the right opportunities, consistency, and lots of patience. But when we open our eyes to what's already in our hand, we are on our way to digging deep toward a life of abundance.

Don't believe me? Grab your spatula, follow me into the kitchen, and let me show you how this principle has worked for me and how it can work for you.

GRAB
YOUR
SPATULA

AT CIA, I LEARNED THAT NOT ONLY IS EVERYTHING IN THE KITCHEN PERISHABLE WITH A LIMITED SHELF LIFE, BUT THERE'S A "QUALITY SHELF LIFE" COMPONENT AS WELL.

A product will only last for a short time, and more importantly, it will be "high quality" product for an even shorter amount of time. This requires controlling food prep, budgeting your orders, and always staying on top of product management.

Unlike a retail establishment, you can't just recover your costs by putting an item on sale the next month or next year when your product is out of style or season. In the food industry, you must aim to sell the raw products or it's money down the drain. Period. On top of that, raw products rarely have a 100 percent yield. After prepping ingredients—slicing, trimming, chopping, peeling, and cooking—you typically lose 15 to 45 percent of the raw product. So, every single little bit really does matter.

Take our Turkey Panini, for example. Coined "The State Bird of Flavortown" by celebrity chef Guy Fieri, the Turkey Panini is our number one seller at my flagship restaurant, Panini Pete's Café & Bakeshoppe in Fairhope, Alabama.

One key ingredient in this sandwich is our homemade garlic aioli. While we only use thirteen grams on each sandwich (yes, that's less than half an ounce), the flavor and balance of this panini would not be the same without it.

On the panini prepping station, we keep this magically delicious aioli in what's called a 1/9th pan (Google it) and use a small spreader to apply the sauce properly. The only problem with this is that the spreader can't fully reach into the corners of the pan. So, just when you think the pan is empty, there's still a good 1 to 1.5 ounces of aioli still clinging to the sides. That's where the mighty spatula comes in to extract the seemingly trivial amount of remaining aioli.

Now, stay with me.

The "insignificant" amount of product is enough for roughly three more panini. Multiply that by four 1/9th pans that we go through every day, seven days a week, and that's an additional twenty-one panini in a given week. That's more than 80 per month, which equates to over 900 panini in a year's time. Need I say more? And this is only one example of one product in single dish. Think of the impact this one single kitchen implement has in saving tens of thousands of dollars from going down the drain each year.

Have you ever wondered how so many restaurants open to lots of fanfare and great reviews only to shut their doors a year later? Carelessness, waste, and a lack of spatula skills are often part of the reason.

When you look at the collective power of seeking out the less appreciated and undervalued items and details, it's mind boggling to look back and consider how much that neglecting the little things ends up costing a business over the years. What's even more tragic is what overlooking the small but significant matters may be costing us in our life.

On the other hand, think of all there is still to gain and the potential for success that's awaiting you if you begin to step into the future, spatula in hand, and dig deep to get the most out of what life has to offer.

Our garlic aioli is essentially derived from the French grandfather to mayonnaise due to the egg yolk, mustard, and citrus. However, its roots are found all over the coastal Mediterranean region. I love this product because it's so versatile. It can be used as a sandwich or panini condiment, a dipping sauce, or even drizzled over a grilled fish or meat dish for an amazing flavor. The aioli base is like a blank canvas that can be flavored and manipulated in countless ways to enhance your dish or sandwich—add roasted jalapeños and cilantro for a south of the border style, roasted peppers for Italian flavoring, Kalamata and oregano for Mediterranean dishes, grilled pineapple and jerk seasoning for a Jamaican twist. The possibilities with this staple recipe are endless!

GARLIC AIOLI

INGREDIENTS:
1 large egg yolk
⅛ cup Dijon mustard
⅛ cup chopped garlic
1 ¾ ounces fresh lime juice
1 fresh lime zest
2 cups vegetable oil
Kosher salt and ground pepper to taste

DIRECTIONS:
In a bowl of a food processor, fitted with
a metal blade, combine the egg, mustard,
garlic, and lime juice.

With the machine running, add the oil
in a steady stream, stop every 30 seconds
until the mixture is pale in color and thick.

Remove from the processor, add zest,
and season to taste.

THE SPATULA'S
RECIPE FOR SUCCESS

Anyone who's worked for a PP Hospitality Group establishment is familiar with the philosophy of success the spatula has inspired. It's a philosophy we've built our entire company around.

I had learned early in my culinary career how important the spatula was to success in the kitchen, but it wasn't until years later that it would translate to a recipe for life.

The lightbulb moment came as I was giving out bonuses to the staff at our annual Christmas party. This is a tradition I carried on from my early days at "The Fish" when I was working for Mike Hurst.

Every year at Christmas, Mike gave the staff a cash bonus. We all appreciated the extra money, especially during the holidays, but the best part was the unique way that Mike delivered "the cheese,"

DO
SOMETHING
SPECIAL

as we called it. One year, it was dollar coins in a Crown Royal bag; the next year, it was crisp five-dollar bills rolled up and placed in a helium balloon (one poor guy accidentally let his go outside). It was always something cool and creative and greatly appreciated.

Flash forward twenty-five years later to when I'm captain of my own ship with Panini Pete's up and running. When the first Christmas rolled around, I knew I wanted to do something special for the staff and honor Mr. Hurst for his impact on my life and career.

Even though the holiday season is a slow time of year for us, I've always managed to scrape up something extra for the team and present it in a fun and memorable way every year—maybe an embroidered logo jacket with some money in the pocket or a hoodie with a stash of dollar coins or two-dollar bills. One year, I even gave the crew some "chocolate and cheese," a little box with candy and some dollar coins.

A few years ago, I decided to give everyone a rubber spatula and wrap some bucks around the handle—just a handy little kitchen tool they could use and some spending money they'd enjoy as well.

As I contemplated my poetic waxing about the importance of the spatula in our industry and the long-term benefits of paying attention to the little

THOSE
SMALL
CONSISTENT
STEPS
WE TAKE

things, I realized just how much the spatula principle paralleled my own life.

As I talked to our team that evening, I really began to articulate how it's those small, consistent steps we take that set us apart in our business. From the fresh ingredients in the dishes we serve, to the hospitality and culture we were creating, the success we were experiencing could all be attributed to our care and attention to even the smallest details.

And looking back, the same has been true of my life— it's the accumulation of many small decisions, actions and opportunities that have, over time, contributed to the overall achievement of leading the full and happy life I've been blessed to live.

DIGGING DEEP DURING
THE EARLY DAYS

I opened Panini Pete's Café & Bakeshoppe in 2006 in the French Quarter of Fairhope, the city's own little Narnia-like shopping and dining district tucked away in the heart of downtown.

It was truly a family affair from day one. I recruited my wife Jodi, a schoolteacher by day (she lasted one week in the kitchen!), my sister Cheryl, my dad who we affectionately called "Butter," and an assistant burger flipper.

When you're going "all in" it requires "all hands on deck!"

Although we began Panini Pete's as a lunch-only concept that opened for business at 11 a.m., I typically arrived between 5 and 7 a.m., depending on the amount of food preparation I needed to complete for the day. We make so much from scratch that it requires time to take the raw ingredients and turn them into ready-to-eat items.

So, early on, when the sales were a bit lean, I was looking to dig deep and get a little more out of the day. How could I "warm up the register" in the morning while prepping and getting ready for lunch?

Being in the Fairhope French Quarter, my first thought was to sell beignets for breakfast. Makes sense, right? I figured I could bust out a batch and sell throughout breakfast hours without getting sidetracked by a full breakfast menu.

Before I even thought about bringing a product to customers, I began research and development. I bought a box of beignet mix to gather a baseline to work from, and I was not at all happy with the results or methodology of these styles of beignets.

I quickly learned I needed a "wet dough" style that I could scoop and fry for quick production so that I could stay focused on lunch prep. That led me to begin playing around with a pâte à choux (the same dough used for eclairs and cream puffs) and getting my egg ratio proper for the consistency that I not only needed but loved when we got to the finished product.

All in all, this experimentation and development was about a six-month process, which was time well spent to get the perfect recipe I was after.

HOSPITALITY GOES A LONG WAY

Once I mastered the recipe, we began to sell them until 11 a.m. every day, or until they sold out. At first, I always had some left over and would "sprinkle" them around town to our local merchants, spreading the love and doing a little covert marketing. I would send out servers to deliver to different merchants on certain days, and if 10:45 a.m. rolled around and their beignets hadn't arrived, they were quick to let me know!

Looking back, that simple act of hospitality went a long way in building relationships with other downtown business owners who have been vital to the success of Panini Pete's over the years.

I remember my beloved landlady, Miss Bessy Montgomery, asking me if I was selling a lot of beignets, and I responded not nearly as many as I was giving away. But word quickly spread, and they became a top seller at Panini Pete's and have earned a reputation far beyond Fairhope.

Another unique thing about our beignets is that we serve them with a lemon wedge on the side. Customers always want to know the story behind this interesting addition.

One day while powdering up some freshly made beignets, I was observing a server cutting lemons for our iced tea service. I was taken back to times when my mom used to make us German pancakes, mostly for special occasions or when we had visitors in our home. These pancakes were kind of like a popover-type batter that were baked in the oven in a hot skillet and always served with copious amounts of drawn butter, powdered sugar, and, yes, lemon. The sour flavor of the lemon complements the sweetness of the powdered sugar and the dough so well.

Of course, I had to try it on my beignets. Everyone went crazy for it, and the rest is history. So, when you're at your local shop eating beignets with lemon, just know that it really started fifteen years ago in small town Alabama.

Earlier this year, due to their popularity, I decided to brand and package our beignet mix so customers can enjoy them at home.

Just don't forget the lemon!

PANINI PETE'S FAMOUS BEIGNET MIX

is available to purchase in all PP Hospitality restaurants, select retailers along the Gulf Coast, and at ChefPaniniPete.com. There's also a how-to video at ChefPaniniPete.com so that you can make our famous beignets in your own kitchen. A portion of the proceeds from the mix will go to benefit the PR Foundation, "doing very special things for very special people."

HIP HIP BEIGNETS

INGREDIENTS:
½ cup water
2 ounces unsalted butter
2 each fresh eggs (beaten)
⅔ cup Panini Pete's Famous Beignet Mix (sifted)

DIRECTIONS:
Sift beignet mix. Place in stainless steel bowl.

Beat eggs, hold in stainless steel bowl.

Chop butter into ½ inch chunks. Place into a small
sauce pot with the water and bring to a rolling boil.
(Have first two ingredients ready.)

Remove from heat. Add beignet mix all at once
and stir with a whisk to combine and form a dough.
(Looks like mashed potatoes.)

Add egg mixture in 3 stages, blending well
with a rubber spatula between each stage.

Scoop using a small #30 scoop into 360-degree oil.
Place it in submerged basket first.

Set timer and release beignets into fryer from basket.
Fry and toss around for approximately 8 minutes.
Drain and place stainless steel bowl. Sprinkle with
powdered sugar. Serve with a lemon wedge.

DIGGING DEEP TO MAXIMIZE YOUR SPATULA'S POTENTIAL

In late 2008, I was contacted by the Food Network about the possibility of Panini Pete's being featured on Guy Fieri's *Diners, Drive-ins and Dives*—a huge opportunity for a small independent locally-owned business like ours.

After five months and numerous phone interviews, we were accepted, and a filming date was set. Holy smokes, what a rush! This was big—very big.

At that moment, as a group, the crew of this little panini shop had accomplished something special. They really believed in what we were doing and worked hard during those early years to lay the groundwork to bring this moment to fruition. They were a dedicated and passionate team, maximizing every single opportunity—they were a crew of Spatula Warriors!

Leading up to production, I began to wonder what would come of this exciting opportunity. Could our team dig down deep and grab all the potential that it might bring? Would going through this window of opportunity open even more doors, or would it just be a single fun experience we'd look back on one day?

We've all watched shows like American Idol and know that so many of the talented competition winners experience a small level of success and a short roller coaster ride of fame and fortune, only to never be heard from again.

On the other hand, there are countless others who got a shot at an audition and didn't win, but who decided to dig deep and make the most out of the opportunity before them. They rose to the occasion, brought value, worked hard, and didn't stop when it was difficult. They kept going, kept digging, and grew a successful life and career.

I knew that I wanted more for our Panini Pete's team than the fifteen minutes of fame a Food Network appearance would bring. I truly wanted to make the most of this unbelievable opportunity and begin to lay a foundation to build even more. How could I maximize the exposure that would come from this moment?

I thought about all that Guy was achieving since being crowned the winner of "Food Network Star."

He had managed to gain a level of success where others who were given the same opportunity had not.

We started filming the segment for the Food Network that spring, and the more I got to know Guy, the more it became evident to me what set him apart from the pack. I saw firsthand how his work ethic, his generosity with others, and his natural ability to dig deep to get the most out of life, family, and business, had allowed him to do so well.

I've seen very talented people who just showed up to read their lines, play the celebrity and move on. But Guy brought value everywhere he went. Over the years, I've seen the value he brings to a show set by engaging in every aspect of production. He challenges himself and his crew to dig deep and deliver an exceptional product. He's always looking for those remaining little bits of goodness within a project—those hidden opportunities. I'd say he's got a golden spatula and may not even know it!

Staying humble and bringing value is so important to building an abundant life. I've seen careers cut short and people never reach their full potential by failing to bring consistent value and benefit to the people and projects around them.

Because our team was willing to give our all and bring value to that first Food Network project, so many more doors have opened for us, including

GIVE
TO THE
WORLD
AROUND
US

more than 20 Food Network appearances, 4 Food Network online video appearances, and over 30 Food & Wine events and shows.

With the prize money from Guy's Food Network Show *Guy's Grocery Games*, I was also able to join with fellow CIA alumni and my good friend Robert Kabakoff to start the PR Foundation, which has helped military veterans, people with special needs, and no-kill animal shelters.

Digging deep is about more than just discovering what we can get out of life and the opportunities it brings us. Digging deep is also about what we can give to the world around us.

In 2011, Guy reached out to me and three other *Diners, Drive-Ins and Dives* alumni chefs —Jeffrey "Stretch" Rumaner, "Gorilla" Rich Bacchi, and Mike "Bossman" Hardin—with an opportunity that would change all of our worlds in ways we could never have imagined.

Guy had been working with Karen Fritz from an organization called Navy Entertainment that brings in some of the top acts in the entertainment arena to boost the morale and spirits of service men and women around the globe. He proposed the idea to send out celebrity chefs (and I use that term loosely!) to entertain the troops through cooking demos and culinary shows.

None of us knew exactly how this would work, but what we did know was that if we could bring these service men and women a little taste of home, it would be a success.

Unlike bands who were brought in to show up for a 20-minute sound check and a 45-minute set and then be on their way, we wanted to bring true value to the lives of these men and women who sacrificed so much. We focused on digging deep to connect with them one-on-one, sharing stories from home and learning about their families while prepping, cooking, and serving the meals. We took over the galley with high energy and excitement, love and appreciation for their sacrifice.

We worked with the culinary specialists and food service officers to create dishes using ingredients they already had on hand in their kitchen and offer some cooking tips and tricks. We cooked thousands of meals that day and were in early and out late, but the hard work was worth every minute. Sure, we signed a few autographs and gave out some swag like a rock band, but we made sure that those deployed men and women were the true celebrities that day.

It's been more than a decade since THE MESSLORDS were born, and during that time, we've served more than 300,000 meals to service men and women all over the world—Japan, Guam, Puerto Rico, Cuba, Spain, Italy, Africa, Bahrain, England, Germany, Belgium, and Romania. We've cooked on aircraft carriers and submarines, and on bases throughout the United States.

Outside of my family, it's been the most gratifying thing I've ever been a part of. It's an honor and privilege to get to serve through this organization.

What started as an opportunity given to four crazy *Diners Drive-In and Dives* alumni has become a successful program with more than twelve chefs volunteering their time and talents to give back. It's been an amazing journey and I am excited to see what the future holds.

Thanks again for another opportunity to dig deep, Guido.

DIGGING DEEP
TO MAKE
AN IMPACT

I want to share with you a story that really shines a light on what can happen when you consistently give back a little—the story of my friend Johnny "The Sheriff" Stewart. My journey with Johnny shows that when you rally a team to apply Spatula Success, great things can happen, lives can be changed, people can be moved to give more, and you can truly appreciate all that you have.

I remember the day this kid who I had never seen before came into Panini Pete's and someone from the kitchen said, "Hey, the Sheriff is here! What's up, Johnny?"

Johnny was a high school kid from the neighborhood who almost everyone knew. He had grown up in Fairhope and at the time was in the special education program at Fairhope High School. He seemed like a good kid, but his appearance was slightly disheveled, to say the least—he definitely could have used a good makeover and a tip or two on his personal hygiene.

Early on in our relationship with Johnny, I remember catching my sister Cheryl giving him free sodas one day, and I said, "If you keep giving Johnny freebies, he'll never leave." Well—16 years later, he still hasn't left, and I couldn't be happier about that.

Johnny would show up on the weekends and make the rounds performing his "sheriff duties." He always talked about helping, but whenever we got busy, he would disappear. By later in that year, he was a fixture around the restaurant, so I started talking to him about cleaning up his appearance a little—shaving some of his whiskers, just as a start. He would always say, "My teachers say the same thing," and he warned me, like he warned them, to "not get his Cajun temper up."

During his Christmas break, Johnny hung around the restaurant, and something just seemed to click with him. He told me he was going to help out the servers a bit, and he certainly did—he bussed tables, he swept the floors, and he ran his butt off. The servers tipped him out and we fed him well.

This led to a good talk about cleaning up his act if he was going to be a "Restaurant Man," and he responded well to it. This new attitude for work really caught on, and Johnny was back at Panini Pete's helping the servers every day during that break.

One of the things that impacted me the most during that time was meeting Johnny's father, George. I had met Johnny's mom briefly before and had seen her around town. Miss Brenda was a wonderful woman and she loved Johnny with every bone in her body. Despite being burdened with some developmental disabilities, she was an amazing person and an incredibly loving mother who gave Johnny everything she could.

I had yet to meet George, but he called the shop mid-morning one day during this Christmas break to chat with me. Loudly and proudly, he said, "I'm George Stewart, Johnny's father, and I want to meet the man my son is working for."

I told him I would love to meet him, too, and to come by the shop anytime, but then he shouted back, "I ain't coming over there! I ain't got no damn legs!" After taking a second to recompose myself, I told him that it was no problem for me to come see him.

George was a Vietnam veteran and lost his legs later in life due to health complications, most likely from exposure to Agent Orange. Obviously, it was tough on him, and his day-to-day life wasn't always necessarily a happy one.

I eventually learned that although Johnny had his own issues to deal with, in many ways he was already the head of the household.

That day, that visit profoundly changed my view and interest in our little Sheriff. Johnny was now part of our family, and I knew he needed our help and support to be his best. What I didn't know was how much he would change my life and the lives of our crew.

I started with buying him a simple dopp kit so he could learn to shave and understand basic daily hygiene practices—simple things most people take for granted having been taught.

Johnny worked hard with us every weekend during high school and came on to the team full time after graduation. I could write an entire book just on my relationship with Johnny. Over the years I've watched him grow into an incredible young man and accomplish awesome things. I was there to see him carry the torch for the Special Olympics and graduate from Fairhope High School (a proud Pirate for life!).

His prom was a particularly memorable event that makes me smile. The year before he graduated, Johnny informed me he was taking his girlfriend to prom and wanted to have their prom dinner at Panini Pete's. I reminded him that we weren't open for dinner to which he replied, "Of course I know that, but I still want to have dinner here. And I want to have spaghetti."

Suffice it to say, a table was set to the nines, and salad, spaghetti, and a beautiful dessert was served with style, as music played in the background. I borrowed a sweet classic car to drive them to the prom and it was a magical night for all of us. It went so well that it was followed up by a repeat performance the next year, but now a table for four was set to accommodate his good friend Dalton and his date. However, Johnny did inform me that I wasn't needed to drive them around because Dalton's dad had ordered them a limo!

It's experiences like these that sparked my desire to find a way to give back more and what eventually led to the birth of the PR Foundation.

Johnny is a legend in and around Fairhope, but he's seen his share of tragedy. He lost his father and eventually his mother as well. His mother's decline was particularly hard on him. Fortunately, Johnny has a community of folks rooting for him and helping him with whatever he needs—his church, some of his former teachers, local residents who have grown to love him, the Fairhope French Quarter family, and, of course, his loyal crew here at Panini Pete's.

Johnny never misses work, he never misses a Fairhope Pirates home football game, and he rarely misses our city council meetings.

I've had a front row seat to so many milestones in Johnny's life, and I'm proud to have been there to help, to support, and to cheer him on with everything he has set his mind to do.

Digging deep is about trying to live your best life and pushing yourself to accomplish all that you are capable of—Johnny has definitely achieved this beyond measure. He's living on his own and married to his childhood sweetheart, Krystal. Johnny is a good, honest, hard-working, and productive member of our community.

Johnny's parents left him a house, but the house was in bad shape. Through generous donations to the PR foundation and with the help of the Baldwin County Homebuilders Association, we've been able to tear down the old house and build a new home for Johnny and Krystal.

Through the PR Foundation, I've been able to dig deep and partner with others who want to dig deep to make an impact in the lives of their neighbors and in their communities in significant ways. I'm so grateful to my good friend Robert Kabakoff for helping turn this vision into a reality.

Robert and I were classmates at the CIA back in the 1980s, and while he was a great friend back then, he's now become just like a brother to me. Robert is a phenomenal chef and has his own consulting firm, RHK Consulting. We also later became business partners in a couple of my restaurants.

While he was president of the CIA Alumni Council, Robert founded the "Run For Your Knives" 5K event during homecoming weekend at the Main Campus in

Hyde Park, which served as a way to promote healthier lifestyles in our industry and helped students with their student loan debt. I joined him as co-chair of the event and, over the years, it really took off. We built it from about 30 participants the first year, which helped raise about $1,000, to well over 200 participants and over $80,000 in scholarships. The winners always receive knife kits, and every student who helps or participates in any way is entered into a raffle where the money is parsed out to help them tackle their student loans.

Because of our friendship all these years, Robert was aware of the legend of Johnny "The Sheriff" Stewart and my hopes to try to create an organization to help give back like we had done with Johnny.

After working together on "Run For Your Knives," Robert suggested that it may be time to try something bigger and help with things beyond student debt.

Robert has always been relentless when it comes to getting things done, so when he has an idea or an intent, it usually comes to fruition—which is one of the things I love about him.

Through that idea and our desire to do something bigger to give back, the PR Foundation was born with our mission and motto—"Doing special things for special people."

We created the non-profit and, as I mentioned earlier, our initial funding was with $20,000 I won from a couple of victories on *Guy's Grocery Games*—so, another shoutout and thanks to Guy Fieri and Food Network.

Robert and I have worked to combine our interests and use the foundation to focus on helping adults with developmental disabilities, military veterans, and no-kill animal shelters. Funds are continuously raised through various events and activities, as well as from our generous friends, family members, and online donors.

I really can't thank Robert enough for being such a driving force in helping to do great things for some great people and causes.

Please check out PRFoundation.net for information on our latest projects and to stay up to date on upcoming events and opportunities. And, of course, if you can, we would appreciate your support, too.

DIGGING DEEP
IS IN
THE DETAILS

Digging deep to achieve a win sometimes means making difficult decisions. When we opened Sunset Pointe, my third restaurant and, at the time, my biggest and "fanciest" restaurant, I knew we had to get it right. It was a huge financial risk, but big rewards rarely come without big risks.

So many locals who weren't aware of my background and years in the industry were wondering what "Panini" was thinking opening an upscale, waterfront seafood joint with fancy food and a proper cocktail bar. What did the sandwich guy know about seafood? I knew not only that we would get it right, but we had to get it right to silence the doubters and satisfy the fans.

There were many examples of digging deep to get this place open and running, but perhaps the toughest and deepest dig came when we decided to delay the opening so that we could train

FOCUS
ON THE
DETAILS

for an additional five days. While we had a great bunch of folks (some of whom are still here to this day) and training was going well, I knew we would hit some bumps.

Opening a restaurant is not just stressful—it's expensive, too. By the time the doors are ready to open, the money spent on renovation, décor, equipment, small wares, tableware, furniture, raw products, beer, wine, liquor and all of the services can total hundreds of thousands of dollars. My decision to delay was a costly one financially.

However, it laid the foundation for our massive triumph. Digging deep and really focusing on the details of our goals for food, service, and hospitality helped to ensure we opened to rave reviews and immense success.

A great example of utilizing under-appreciated product to gain tremendous value is one that has really put Sunset Pointe on the map—our Gulf Snapper Throats. It's also an incredible example of seafood sustainability.

The "throat" of the snapper is located between the ever-so-popular filet and the gills. It's often ignored because it can be difficult to use, but it's arguably the best meat on the fish. In Japan, the Hamachi collar is a coveted dish. It's moist and delicious and very precious in that culture.

At Sunset Pointe, we season the Red Snapper collar with our version of a Cajun topping and grill over a flame for approximately 4 or 5 minutes per side depending on the size of the fish. After the collar comes off the grill, we baste the fish with a simple garlic compound butter and serve with charred lemon. And it is delicious.

The Gulf Snapper Throats dish is our number one selling entrée at Sunset Pointe.

Think about that for a moment. By recognizing the potential value in one single product—one that's been mostly ignored and discarded—we brought more popularity and prof-it to our restaurant and created a dish that our customers love. Not to mention how utilizing more of the fish has lessened the impact on the Gulf's precious Red Snapper population.

GULF SNAPPER THROAT
GARLIC BUTTER

INGREDIENTS:
2 sticks unsalted butter
1 lemon lightly zested
⅛ cup of olive oil
¼ cup minced garlic
¼ teaspoon freshly ground black pepper
¼ teaspoon salt
⅛ cup finely chopped parsley
¼ cup lemon juice

DIRECTIONS:
Combine all ingredients except parsley in sauce pot
on low heat. Heat until butter is translucent.

Remove from stove and whisk fresh parsley
into mixture. Makes 2 ½ cups.

Season snapper throats with salt and pepper or your
favorite seasonings, grill 4-6 minutes on each side,
and apply garlic butter.

DIGGING DEEP
TO GET TO THE
NEXT LEVEL

Digging deep means regularly assessing where you are and where you want to go. It's being aware of changes around you and adapting to those changes in order to continue to grow and be successful.

We had been operating a second Panini Pete's Café & Bakeshoppe in downtown Mobile since 2012 and were on track to be outpacing the Fairhope location in sales within two years. Located in a true business district, we were slammed for about an hour and a half during the lunch hour rush but slow the rest of the day.

As efforts were put into revitalizing the downtown area of Mobile, a new nightlife scene began to emerge. People were looking for a place to relax and have a drink after work and families were frequenting the downtown area for dinner more often.

As a restaurateur and businessman, I began to wonder how we could capitalize on this evolving market. There was obviously a need for more than just a place to eat lunch. The question was, how do we adapt to meet the changing market? Do we extend our hours? Expand our menu?

After careful consideration, we decided to completely rebrand. It was a tough decision to change what had become an iconic brand and, in all honesty, part of my identity. What started out as the name of a restaurant had quite literally become who I was to so many people—"Panini Pete." So, when I made the choice to shut down the Mobile location, I had to be careful not to let my ego get in the way, knowing that some would perceive this rebranding as a failure. But nothing could be further from the truth. I had made the choice to dig deep and take a risk based on changing circumstances that would eventually catapult our entire restaurant group to another level.

We closed Panini Pete's doors in January 2019 and went to work with the research and renovation.

I really wanted this to be an opportunity to flex some culinary muscle and create something unique. The new concept would feature lunch, dinner, and cocktails. I wanted to incorporate the history of Mobile and pay tribute to the restaurants that had come before—to tell a story through both the venue and the menu.

I also wanted to appeal to a younger generation and create a cool brand that would do well in the merch market. I wanted the new brand to intrigue customers and offer a special experience they couldn't find anywhere else.

After six months of digging deep to make this dream a reality, Squid Ink Eclectic Eats & Drinks opened in June 2019.

If you're familiar with its history, you'll know that Mobile is the oldest city in Alabama and spent years under French, British, and Spanish rule. I wanted the menu to reflect all of those influences and still be palatable to our clientele. So, on our menu you'll find dishes like our Spanish S.O.S. (Squid on a Shingle) right next to our London Calling Fish n Chips and our French 75-inspired Black Cadillac cocktail—all a nod to Mobile's rich and diverse heritage.

BLACK CADILLAC
COCKTAIL

TOOLS:
Coupe Glass
Shaker
Strainer

INGREDIENTS:
1 ½ ounces Bombay Sapphire
½ ounce Blueberry Syrup (recipe next page)
½ ounce Ink Syrup (recipe next page)
¾ ounce Lemon Juice
½ ounce Champagne

DIRECTIONS:
Chill coupe glass.

Place all ingredients into shaker.

Top with champagne and garnish
with dehydrated lemon.

BLUEBERRY SYRUP

INGREDIENTS:
1 small pack of blueberries (roughly 6 ounces)
18 ounces water
6 ounces sugar

DIRECTIONS:
In a saucepan, combine blueberries and water, heat to boil. While the mixture is still hot, lightly crush the blueberries with a large spoon, just enough to break all of the skin on the berries. Let the blueberries steep for 20 minutes. Strain blueberries out of the water mixture and stir in sugar until it is fully dissolved.
Let syrup cool to room temperature before storing in refrigerator. Yields roughly 22 fluid ounces.

• • •

SQUID INK SYRUP

INGREDIENTS:
15 ounces sugar
15 ounces water
2 teaspoons ink

DIRECTIONS:
Combine ink and sugar in quart container.
Boil water in saucepan, remove from heat and allow to cool slightly so it won't melt the quart container.
Carefully pour water into quart container and stir until sugar dissolves and squid ink is fully incorporated. The mixture may require a hand blender to break up tiny ink particles.

DIGGING DEEP
DURING LIFE'S
UNEXPECT-ED'S

If you live a life of digging deep every day, you may find yourself stumbling into opportunities.

I was not planning on acquiring another restaurant brand when the opportunity to purchase Ed's Seafood Shed was presented to me. Ed's had been successful for about a decade but had experienced a steady downturn in recent years. The sales weren't great (but they were nothing to sneeze at either) and the building needed a lot of work. I knew the brand still had value and a loyal customer base. If I could acquire the real estate in addition to the restaurant, then it would be a smart deal for me. More importantly, if our team could dig deep and do what we did best, I knew we could bring life back to the Ed's brand.

We set out to do just that in October of 2017. It was a substantial investment of time, money, and training, and I had to keep my eyes on our long-term goals.

It's important to understand the balance between digging deep to invest and not overextending. We had to prioritize our investments and put a plan together for sustainable success.

We had to listen and pay attention to customers whose loyalty had been to the previous owners. We had to prove to the staff that we knew what we were doing and that we were willing to dig deep and help them get it done. There was a status quo that had been followed for so long and we had to be clear that we were going to expect more from them. We weren't there to throw the baby out with the bath water but to take the kid to college, so to speak. I wanted to bring progress but also preservation to what had been a local mainstay for so many years.

Going back to the fundamentals of running a business and paying attention to the bottom line and holding true to the intangibles like hospitality and hard work that had led to our success would be crucial if we were going to turn this ship around. And we did.

It's not been smooth sailing all the time, but we've stayed the course and we've experienced success even during some rough waters—literally.

Ed's overlooks Mobile Bay on what locals call the "Causeway" between Spanish Fort and Mobile, where it's not uncommon to have to close during a high tide that floods the parking lot. Located right in the middle of that infamous "cone of uncertainty," we have to batten down the hatches pretty regularly during hurricane season.

On top of braving the winds and waves, an electrical fire broke out last year ravaging Ed's and forcing us to shut down for a period of six months to a year as we look to rebuild.

And if flooding and fires weren't apocalyptic enough, cue the plagues.

At the writing of this book, the Covid-19 global pandemic has brought unprecedented challenges, especially to those of us in the hospitality industry. In a business where our main function is to bring people together, we were shut down overnight with no answers as to what the future would look like for our business.

I remember right before the stay-at-home order was issued in March of 2020, we were getting ready for what is typically our Fairhope restaurants' busiest week of the year, our city's annual arts and crafts festival. We learned quickly just how devastating this pandemic had the potential to be when we brought in only 3% in sales compared to the sales of that same week in previous years. It was easy to let panic set in at that point.

What does it mean to dig deep when so much is out of your control? Sure, relief was coming but no one knew how long that would be or how long this pandemic would last. There were so many unknowns. We had to shut down all our restaurants and lay off 150 employees.

It's during times like these that it is so important to have a community of support around you, especially mentors. I was fortunate to be able to call on fellow restaurateurs across the country for advice.

Our team rallied together to help each other. Communication was key during this uncertain time. We provided meals and gift cards to our staff and made sure everyone had toilet paper and household supplies as shelves became emptier by the day.

Even as we've moved forward and reopened, we're still dealing with the effects of the pandemic with supply chain problems and labor shortages.

But during times of crisis, you can always choose to dig deep to rise above adversity, grow, and come out even better on the other side.

During this pandemic, for example, we've been forced to become better trainers because some of our staff has had to step in to do jobs they weren't originally hired to do. We've had to learn to become better recruiters in a limited workforce. We've had to become better analyzers of the systems that have been in place and fine tune them so that we can meet the current challenges.

If you dig deep—yes, even in adversity—you can gain invaluable tools that you never would have otherwise. It's in times like this, when everything you've built is being tested, that you learn what you're made of and the integrity of what you've spent your life building.

And, as of today, I'm grateful that we're still standing—continuing to dig deep one day at a time.

DIGGING DEEP
DURING
DIFFICULTY

One of my favorite quotes that I call to mind when the stress of the business starts to weigh heavy on me comes from the late Mike "Bossman" Hardin of Hodad's in San Diego. Mike always said, when referring to what we do every day in the restaurant industry, "It's not life and death... just lunch and dinner."

That perspective hit home for me, quite literally, when my wife Jodi was diagnosed with breast cancer in 2017. When you get that kind of news, it's as if your world comes to a standstill and you start to reevaluate what's most important in your life. My family is everything to me and so I decided then and there that Jodi's wellbeing came first, even if that meant stepping back from the restaurants for the time being. I was the only person who could be a husband to Jodi and a dad to my kids as our family walked through this difficult time.

I knew I had to dig deep to stay strong for myself so that I could support Jodi. Whether that meant venting my fears and anxiety to a trusted friend or taking a walk to get alone and pray, I knew I had to take care of myself so I could take care of my wife.

I also knew that because of the groundwork we had laid and the team structure in which we operate, the restaurants were set up to take care of themselves. And, if there were a few breakdowns along the way, we could regroup and fix those later. Again, like Bossman said, "It's not life and death...just lunch and dinner."

While we had dealt with challenges related to the business over the years, when circumstances take an unexpected turn for the worse or tragedy strikes in our work family, it's an altogether different thing.

It's during these tough times—when life delivers unexpected blows that shake you down to your core— that you can decide to give up, or you can choose to dig deep and muster every bit of fight and faith that you have left to keep going.

You won't be able to do it alone—we were never meant to do it alone. We need each other. That's why one of our top priorities in the business is to cultivate a culture of community in our work family.

When hard times inevitably come your way, you will need a support system to help shoulder your struggles. Find your people and lock arms with them. Ask for help when you need it.

The future that's waiting on the other side of whatever it is you may be facing, is worth the fight to push through.

DIGGING DEEP TO BUILD SUCCESSFUL TEAMS

Not only do you need your people when life gets tough, but you will also need a team around you to reach the goals you've set and the future you want to create. It may sound cliché, but no man is an island. Digging deep to reach your full potential will require help from others. In my case, I believe that building a successful team around me has been the ultimate key to our success.

When I started out in my culinary career, I could never have imagined what the future would hold or what I could achieve. It's often someone else who recognizes our potential before we can see it in ourselves. It was my operating partner Nick who first saw the entrepreneurial drive in me.

Nick and I met in 1989 when we were both working at a local restaurant chain in Tuscaloosa, Alabama. Our career journeys took us in different directions but, as it often does, life brought us full circle and our paths crossed again 25 years later. We reconnected in 2014 and set out to build a business and hospitality brand like no other.

Nick and I are yin and yang, which is why we work so well together. We each understand our lane of business as it relates to using the spatula philosophy to get the most out of everything that we set our mind to do.

The hospitality industry is in the business of bringing people together. From curating an enjoyable dining experience for our customers to cultivating an environment where our work family can thrive, *people* are at the center of everything we do. That's why one of our slogans is "We've Never Met a Stranger."

We want every person who visits one of our restaurants to feel like they're one of the family.

Developing that kind of environment starts long before the first customer walks through the door. It starts with developing that sense of family and comradery among your team.

Identifying talent is important and determining how those skills contribute to the success of the entire team is critical. Whether it's their personality, work ethic, speed, ability to focus, crisis management, timeliness, adaptability, or reliability, developing a winning lineup starts with learning where each player brings the most value to the team.

Operationally, every position and function on the team must have guidelines and methods. From recipes and timelines to walk-throughs and checklists, there must be a base template of discipline to follow.

For example, you may be able to cook an amazing dish, but can you produce the exact same dish the exact same way 75 times a day 6 days a week?

You can't have any level of achievement without a consistent plan, and you must commit to the time, money, and work it takes to see that training through to the end.

The old (but often still used) methods of "work with so-and-so over there and they'll show you the ropes" is lazy and ineffective, especially if your team is not properly trained from the beginning.

Take the time and money to write out the details of the job or the role, and then be sure to elaborate on the whys of what they are doing, as well as how it affects not only their success but the overall success of the team.

I believe one of our main responsibilities when it comes to building a successful team is to dig deep to plant and grow people. That's why our training doesn't just revolve around the task at hand, but also emphasizes the life skills and standards necessary to win in your life's pursuits.

PLANT
AND GROW
PEOPLE

We are always striving to move our team forward in mastering their role and preparing for the next level. In our industry, the bulk of the team is passing through for a short time—maybe six months to a couple of years while they're in school. Other than our corporate office and our management staff, we are lucky to keep a small corps of pros on our team. We're a lot like a college sports program, in that we must always be coaching, developing, and recruiting. And just like a great college sports program, if you have a reputation for developing superstars, other companies will actively try to recruit your team members to join theirs.

We realize that we won't be the final stop for most of our staff. We're always looking for ways to keep an employee for the rest of their work life, but it's just as important to us to help each one grow and reach their next step in pursuit of their personal goals. That may mean helping them talk to a banker about opening their own restaurant, or it may mean guiding them in the direction of another career field altogether.

We are more focused on planting and growing people than we are the harvest. If we continue to dig deep, then the harvest will flourish and everyone wins.

We are passionate about digging deep to invest in the next generation. That's why we've partnered with organizations like the Gateway Initiative, our home county's workforce development program, and ProStart, a nationwide, two-year high school program that teaches culinary techniques and management skills to students interested in the hospitality industry.

Not only are these programs great recruitment tools for our industry, but it gives us the opportunity to mentor the next generation and make a difference in the trajectory of their life in a positive way.

It's not just today's youth that need mentors—we all do. Age is just a number and a perspective, and there is always more growing to do no matter how much life experience you have under your belt.

We're always looking for people to follow and learn from who share our similar philosophy but who are smarter than us. This is what has allowed us to venture into so many business opportunities outside of the hospitality industry.

If you invest in those around you and continually invest in your own growth, you'll be amazed at the abundance waiting for those who choose to live a life of digging deep.

GRAB YOUR
SPATULA
AND LET'S
GO!

STANDING OUT ON THE FLIGHT DECK OF THE "BIG E," THAT DAY WAS A MOMENT OF EPIPHANY FOR ME. It opened my eyes to see how digging deep had made all the difference in my life, and it gave me the blueprint for building the future I desired.

I hope that in reading *Spatula Success*, you have had a few lightbulb moments of your own.

There are countless books on how to achieve success. And the definition of a successful life is going to be different depending on who you ask. But no matter what success looks like to you, I believe we all share an innate desire to know that we're reaching our full potential and that we're impacting the world around us. I hope that through reading this book, you've come to see that the success found in digging deep isn't just about acquiring wealth or status, checking off a list of personal goals, or racking up awards or trophies – which are all admirable things to aspire to do. The life of abundance that comes from digging deep is ultimately one of fulfillment and meaning, one that inspires and enriches the lives of others.

It's my hope that in sharing my story, you'll begin to consider what digging deep looks like in your own life. Are you paying attention to the small details that others often neglect? Are you bringing value to the place where you currently find yourself? Are you making the most of the opportunities in front of you? Remember, the little things matter, and getting to the future you're dreaming of starts with digging deep, working hard, and doing good right where you are today. When you do, you'll be amazed at where life will take you and, even more importantly, how many people will be impacted along the way.

ACKNOWLEDGMENTS

First and foremost, I have to thank the late and great Mike Hurst. Mike was an amazingly successful restaurateur, accomplished professor of hospitality management, and former president of the National Restaurant Association. Working for Mike during my high school years is where I caught the "restaurant bug." He encouraged me to attend the CIA and always took good care of the staff at the 15th St. Fisheries for Christmas—a very generous and kind act that would later inspire me to do something similar for my crew at Panini Pete's and eventually lead to the very first "Spatula Speech." I miss you, Big Mike!

Secondly, I want to thank my many chef instructors and the amazing culture at the Culinary Institute of America. Without that foundation and education nothing I've accomplished to date would have been possible. I learned the importance of high standards and attention to detail there, as well as how useful a spatula could be in "digging deep" to survive in our industry.

I must also give massive credit to my lady, my love, my wife Jodi. She has been by my side through the many phases and ups and downs of my restaurant career. I have witnessed firsthand and learned from watching her—from her amazing ability and love of teaching special education to her raising our two children Arnold and Isabella, and her strength and spirit while waging her victorious battle against breast cancer. She inspires and supports me always.

Thanks so much to Stephanie and Keith Glines. If you are reading this, it's a miracle. I'm grateful to Keith for believing in me and this concept enough to go along on this project and all our many journeys still in progress. And for Steph, making sense of my words and story to effectively articulate it while keeping it all in "Pete Speak" (yet without so much cursing!)—that was a monster challenge. Love you guys.

A huge thanks to Mr. Nicholas V. Dimario, my business partner and long lost "brother from another mother." Thanks for all you have done to help make PP Hospitality so successful and, more importantly, a company that always digs deep, not only to succeed but to lead, teach, grow, and nurture our teams. You're a true hospitality bad-ass leader, my brutha!

And, of course, so much gratitude goes out to the one and only Guy "Guido" Fieri! Thank you for inspiring me to push hard and think big. Having a front row seat for the last 14 years to watch the rise of your empire has been an unforgettable experience. The excitement of running around trying to keep pace with this "Guy" is like being surrounded by your best friends on the 50-yard line at the Super Bowl…or courtside at the NBA finals…before heading backstage at a rock concert…all rolled into one. I think you get the point—it's been a wild ride! And the food is great too! Thanks for letting me be part of so many incredible adventures. Without so much Food Network exposure no one would buy this book anyway. Love ya and "Roll Tide," Guido!

ABOUT CHEF "PANINI" PETE BLOHME

Chef "Panini" Pete Blohme has been fascinated with the art of cooking since he began working in restaurants at the age of 14. After graduating from the Culinary Institute of America, Hyde Park, NY in 1986, Pete spent more than 20 years in the restaurant business learning from some of the best in the industry. He opened Panini Pete's Café & Bakeshoppe in Fairhope, AL, in 2006, and has spent the past 17 years building a restaurant company and hospitality brand that today operates four award-winning establishments on the Gulf Coast.

Pete has headlined with Guy Fieri on his Live Road Show performing in 25-plus Road Shows and been featured on a host of Food Network shows such as *Diners, Drive-Ins and Dives*; *Guy's Grocery Games*; *Guy's Big Bite* and *The Great Food Truck Race with Tyler Florence*, as well as CMT's *Sweet Home Alabama*.

Always looking to dig deep and give back, Pete is a founding member of The Messlords, a group of passionate chefs that travel around the world, cooking and entertaining American troops, as well as co-founder of the PR Foundation that works to help veterans, adults with developmental disabilities, and no-kill animal shelters.

Spatula Success is his first book.

Connect with Pete on social media and by subscribing to his podcast, "The Raw Ingredients," available on all streaming platforms.

Panini Pete Hospitality Group, LLC.

"We Put Real Food in our Food"

panini
Pete's
Cafe & Market

SUNSET POINTE

FAIRHOPE
ALABAMA

MESSLORDS

FORK FULL OF FREEDOM

MOB TOWN
PROPER

ED'S
SEAFOOD SHED

SPANISH FORT, ALABAMA

CHEF PETE BLOHME

RAW
INGREDIENT'S
PODCAST

SQUID INK

ECLECTIC

EATS & DRINKS

FAIRHOPE
Squeeze

JUICE BAR · FRUTERIA

CPSIA information can be obtained
at www.ICGtesting.com
Printed in the USA
JSHW030011231122
33627JS00004B/12/J